A Sweet Bundle of Love

HOLLY POND HILL
BY SUSAN WHEELER

HARVEST HOUSE PUBLISHERS
Eugene, Oregon

A Sweet Bundle of Love
Text copyright © 2001 by Harvest House Publishers
Eugene, OR 97402

ISBN 0-7369-0513-8

Design and production by Garborg Design Works, Minneapolis, Minnesota

Children are the hands
by which we take hold of heaven.

HENRY WARD BEECHER

There is one order of beauty
which seems made to turn heads...
It is a beauty like that of
kittens, or very small downy ducks
making gentle rippling noises with
their soft bills, or babies just
beginning to toddle...

GEORGE ELIOT

From small beginnings come great things.

AUTHOR UNKNOWN

A new baby is like the beginning of all things—wonder, hope, a dream of possibilities.

EDA LESHAN

A BABY...ONE OF THE MOST BEAUTIFUL MIRACLES IN LIFE, ONE OF THE GREATEST JOYS WE CAN EVER KNOW, AND ONE OF THE REASONS WHY THERE IS A LITTLE EXTRA SUNSHINE, LAUGHTER AND HAPPINESS IN YOUR WORLD TODAY.

AUTHOR UNKNOWN

Father asked us what was God's noblest work. Anna said men, but I said babies. Men are often bad, but babies never are.

LOUISA MAY ALCOTT

For you created my inmost being; you knit me together in my mother's womb.

I praise you because I am fearfully and wonderfully made; your works are wonderful, I know that full well.

My frame was not hidden from you when I was made in the secret place. When I was woven together in the depths of the earth, your eyes saw my unformed body. All the days ordained for me were written in your book before one of them came to be.

THE BOOK OF PSALMS

9

"But where do babies come from, then?"
asked the girl.

"Why, an angel from heaven brings them under
his cloak, but no man can see him; and that's
why we never know when he brings them."

At that moment there was a rustling in
the branches of the willow tree, and the
children folded their hands and looked at one
another: it was certainly the angel coming with
the baby. They took each other's hand, and at
that moment the door of one of the houses
opened, and the neighbour appeared.

"Come in, you two," she said. "See what the
stork has brought. It is a little brother."

HANS CHRISTIAN ANDERSEN
WHAT THE MOON SAW

A baby will make love stronger,
days longer, nights shorter, bankroll smaller,
home happier, clothes shabbier, the past
forgotten, and the future worth living for.

AUTHOR UNKNOWN

11

WE NEVER KNOW THE LOVE OF A PARENT TILL

WE BECOME PARENTS OURSELVES.

HENRY WARD BEECHER

*A baby is
God's opinion that
life should go on.*

CARL SANDBURG

Mrs. Weston, with her baby on her
knee, indulging in such reflections
as these, was one of the happiest
women in the world. If any thing
could increase her delight, it was
perceiving that the baby would soon
have outgrown its first set of caps.

JANE AUSTEN
EMMA

13

Sleep my child and peace attend thee,
All through the night.
Guardian angels God will send thee,
All through the night.
Soft the drowsy hours are creeping,
Hill and vale in slumber sleeping,
I my loving vigil keeping,
All through the night.

AUTHOR UNKNOWN

Babies are such a nice way to start people.

DON HEROLD

Give a Little
Love to a Child
& You Get a
Great Deal Back

Children are God's way of

The baby was a year old, and plump and dimpled, and fond of me, and never could get enough of hauling on my tail, and hugging me, and laughing out its innocent happiness.

MARK TWAIN
A DOG'S TALE

elling you tomorrow is beautiful.

For this child I prayed and the Lord has given me my petition which I asked of Him.

THE BOOK OF FIRST SAMUEL

Blessings for Baby

We are sprinkled from morning
till night with the dew of God's grace.

—Paul Hortepeter

Children are our most valuable natural resource.

HERBERT HOOVER

THE LAUGHTER OF A CHILD IS THE LIGHT OF A HOUSE.

AUTHOR UNKNOWN

We can't form our children on
our own concepts; we must take
them and love them as God
gives them to us.

GOETHE

We find delight in
the beauty and
happiness of
children that makes
the heart too big
for the body.

RALPH WALDO EMERSON

CHILDREN ARE A
POOR MAN'S RICHES.

ENGLISH PROVERB

21

"Mothers see something extraordinary in their children, that is ordained by nature," said Yulia. "A mother will stand for hours together by the baby's cot looking at its little ears and eyes and nose, and fascinated by them. If any one else kisses her baby the poor thing imagines that it gives him immense pleasure. And a mother talks of nothing but her baby. I know that weakness in mothers, and I keep watch over myself, but my Olga really is exceptional. How she looks at me when I'm nursing her! How she laughs! She's only eight months old, but, upon my word, I've never seen such intelligent eyes in a child of three."

ANTON CHEKHOV
THREE YEARS

Jesus said, "Let the little children come to me,
and do not hinder them, for the kingdom
of heaven belongs to such as these."

THE BOOK OF MATTHEW

A CRADLE SONG

Sweet dreams, form a shade
O'er my lovely infant's head;
Sweet dreams of pleasant streams
By happy, silent, moony beams.

Sweet sleep, with soft down
Weave thy brows an infant crown.
Sweet sleep, Angel mild,
Hover o'er my happy child.

Sweet smiles, in the night
Hover over my delight;
Sweet smiles, mother's smiles,
All the livelong night beguiles.

Sweet moans, dovelike sighs,
Chase not slumber from thy eyes.
Sweet moans, sweeter smiles,
All the dovelike moans beguiles.

Sleep, sleep, happy child,
All creation slept and smil'd;
Sleep, sleep, happy sleep,
While o'er thee thy mother weep.

Sweet babe, in thy face
Holy image I can trace.
Sweet babe, once like thee,
Thy Maker lay and wept for me,

Wept for me, for thee, for all,
When He was an infant small.
Thou His image ever see,
Heavenly face that smiles on thee,

Smiles on thee, on me, on all;
Who became an infant small.
Infant smiles are His own smiles;
Heaven and earth to peace beguiles.

WILLIAM BLAKE

"God sends children for another purpose than merely to keep up the race—to enlarge our hearts."

MARY HOWITT

Train a child in the way he should go, and when he is old he will not turn from it.

THE BOOK OF PROVERBS

The watchful mother tarries nigh,
though sleep has closed her
infant's eyes.

JOHN KEBLE

**A CHILD IS A BEAM OF SUNLIGHT FROM THE
INFINITE AND ETERNAL, WITH POSSIBILITIES OF
VIRTUE AND VICE—BUT AS YET UNSTAINED.**

LYMAN ABBOTT

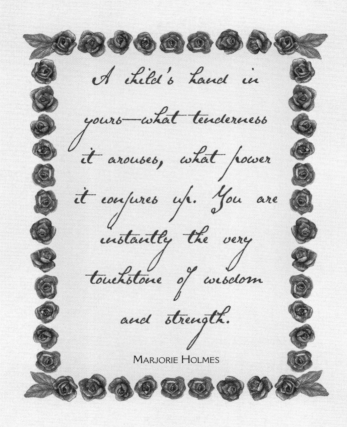

A child's hand in
yours—what tenderness
it arouses, what power
it conjures up. You are
instantly the very
touchstone of wisdom
and strength.

MARJORIE HOLMES

YOU ARE LOVED JUST
AS YOU ARE RIGHT THIS
VERY MOMENT. THE
WORLD HAS BECOME
MORE WONDERFUL JUST
BECAUSE YOU ARE HERE.

DEBBY BOONE

If one feels the need of something grand,
something infinite, something that makes one
feel aware of God, one need not go far to find
it. I think that I see something deeper, more
infinite, more eternal than the ocean in the
expression of the eyes of a little baby when it
wakes in the morning and coos or laughs
because it sees the sun shining on its cradle.

VINCENT VAN GOGH

31

Two dimpled hands,
Ten tiny toes,
One rosebud mouth,
One snubby nose.

A pair of bright eyes,
Twin pools of blue,
Sunshine and showers
Reflecting through.

A soft gurgling laugh,
An innocent smile,
A good healthy yell
Once in a while.

I'm lost in the wonder
Of life's greatest joy
As I gaze on the face
Of my wee sleeping boy.

MILLY WALTON

Hush, my dear! Lie still and slumber;
Holy angels guard thy bed!
Heavenly blessings without number
Gently falling on thy head.

How much better thou'rt attended
Than the Son of God could be,
When from heaven He descended
And became a child like thee!

Mayest thou live to know and fear Him
Trust and love Him all thy days;
Then go dwell forever near Him
See His face, and sing His praise.

ISAAC WATTS

May your father and mother be glad

Sing a song of baby,
So happy that you're here!
Sing a song of carefree days,
For you're so very dear.

PAUL KORTEPETER

may she who gave you birth rejoice!

THE BOOK OF PROVERBS

A BABY IS AN INESTIMABLE
BLESSING AND BOTHER.

MARK TWAIN

Two little eyes to look to God,
Two little ears to hear His Word,
Two little feet to walk His ways,
Hands to serve Him all my days.

One little tongue to speak His truth,
One little heart for Him in youth,
Take them, O Jesus, let them be
Always willing, true to Thee.

AUTHOR UNKNOWN

Every baby comes as evidence that God
still dreams of Eden.

CALVIN MILLER

Lo, children are a heritage of the Lord: and the fruit of the womb is his reward. As arrows are in the hand of a mighty man; so are children of the youth. Happy is the man that hath his quiver full of them.

THE BOOK OF PSALMS (KJV)

Every baby needs a lap.

HENRY ROBIN

Making a decision to have a child— it's momentous. It is to decide forever to have your heart go walking around outside your body.

ELIZABETH STONE

DON'T FORGET THAT COMPARED TO A GROWN-UP PERSON EVERY BABY IS A GENIUS. THINK OF THE CAPACITY TO LEARN! THE FRESHNESS, THE TEMPERAMENT, THE WILL OF A BABY A FEW MONTHS OLD!

MAY SARTON

A baby is something you carry inside you for
nine months, in your arms for three years and
in your heart till the day you die.

MARY MASON

Welcoming a newborn baby is somehow
absolute, truer and more binding than
any other experience that life has to offer.

MARILYN FRENCH

OF ALL THE JOYS

THAT LIGHTEN

SUFFERING EARTH,

WHAT JOY IS

WELCOMED LIKE A

NEWBORN CHILD?

CAROLINE NORTON

I don't know
whether this will
be a boy or a girl...
But this child was
invited into the
world and it will be
a wonderful child.

MARGARET BOURKE-WHITE

*There was a star danced,
and under that was I born.*

WILLIAM SHAKESPEARE

A NEW LIFE BEGUN,

LIKE FATHER, LIKE SON.

LIKE ONE, LIKE THE OTHER,

LIKE DAUGHTER, LIKE MOTHER.

AUTHOR UNKNOWN

A baby is...a rose with all its sweetest leaves yet folded.

LORD BYRON

I love these little people, and it is
not a slight thing when they, who
are so fresh from God, love us.

CHARLES DICKENS

Baby Feet

Tell me, what is half so sweet
As a baby's tiny feet,
Pink and dainty as can be,
Like a coral from the sea?
Talk of jewels strung in rows,
Gaze upon those little toes,
Fairer than a diadem,
With the mother kissing them!

It is morning and she lies
Uttering her happy cries,
While her little hands reach out
For the feet that fly about.
Then I go to her and blow
Laughter out of every toe;
Hold her high and let her place
Tiny footprints on my face.

Little feet that do not know
Where the winding roadways go,
Little feet that never tire,
Feel the stones or trudge the mire,
Still too pink and still too small
To do anything but crawl,
Thinking all their wanderings fair,
Filled with wonders everywhere.

Little feet, so rich with charm,
May you never come to harm.
As I bend and proudly blow
Laughter out of every toe,
This pray, that God above
Shall protect you with His love,
And shall guide those little feet
Safely down life's broader street.

EDGAR GUEST

My baby boy is changing far too quickly,
growing too fast. But there is still something
like angel dust glistening in his downy hair,
and there are times I find myself wondering
if he isn't somehow a message sent to me from
the world that dreamed him up. Some nights,
watching him sleep, I feel certain we are both
cradled in a stronger embrace, and I cannot
help but believe that he and I—all of us—
are meant for more than this world.

CAROLYN ARENDS
LIVING THE QUESTIONS